From Zero to Creative Hero: Beginning Your Journey with Adobe Creative Studio

Chapter 1: Introduction to Adobe Creative Studio

1.1: The Power of Creativity

1.2: Exploring the Adobe Creative Studio Suite

1.3: Setting Up Your Workspace

Chapter 2: Adobe Photoshop – Image Editing and Manipulation

2.1: Navigating the Photoshop Interface

2.2: Working with Layers and Selections

2.3: Color Correction and Retouching Techniques

2.4: Creating Composites and Applying Effects

2.5: Exporting and Optimizing Images

Chapter 3: Adobe Illustrator – Vector Art and Illustration

3.1: Understanding the Illustrator Workspace

3.2: Drawing with the Pen and Pencil Tools

3.3: Working with Colors, Gradients, and Patterns

3.4: Typography and Text Effects

3.5: Designing Logos and Icons

Chapter 4: Adobe InDesign – Layout and Publication Design

4.1: An Introduction to InDesign's Interface

4.2: Creating and Managing Pages and Master Pages

4.3: Working with Text, Frames, and Graphics

4.4: Typography and Styling in InDesign

4.5: Preparing Files for Print and Digital Publishing

Chapter 5: Adobe Premiere Pro – Video Editing and Production

5.1: Exploring the Premiere Pro Workspace

5.2: Importing and Organizing Media

5.3: Basic Editing Techniques and Transitions

5.4: Adding Titles, Effects, and Color Correction

Preface

The world of digital creativity is vast, ever-evolving, and full of potential. Whether you're a budding designer, a seasoned creative professional, or simply someone who wants to harness the power of creativity in your personal or professional life, mastering Adobe Creative Studio is a valuable investment in your skill set.

"From Zero to Creative Hero: Beginning Your Journey with Adobe Creative Studio" was born out of a passion for empowering individuals to unleash their creative potential. This book aims to serve as a comprehensive guide, providing a solid foundation in the core Adobe Creative Studio applications, and offering practical tips and techniques to help you elevate your creative work.

Throughout this book, you will explore the essential tools and features of Photoshop, Illustrator, InDesign, Premiere Pro, and After Effects. You will learn how to navigate each application's interface, customize your workspace, and streamline your workflow. From image editing and vector illustration to layout design, video editing, and motion graphics, this book covers a wide range of skills and techniques to help you create stunning visuals and engaging content.

In addition to mastering the technical aspects of Adobe Creative Studio, this book will also inspire you to think creatively and approach problem-solving with an open mind. You will discover the power of storytelling, develop your artistic voice, and learn how to showcase your work effectively in a professional portfolio.

It is our hope that "From Zero to Creative Hero" will serve as a valuable resource on your journey to becoming a confident, versatile, and innovative creative professional. We encourage you to experiment, make mistakes, and embrace the creative process as you explore the possibilities that Adobe Creative Studio has to offer.

Let's embark on this exciting journey together. The world of digital creativity awaits!

Happy creating!

Chapter 1: Introduction to Adobe Creative Studio

1.1: The Power of Creativity

Creativity is the driving force behind innovation, problem-solving, and personal expression. It plays a vital role in various industries, from design and advertising to technology and education. By harnessing the power of creativity, individuals and organizations can develop unique solutions, captivate audiences, and forge new paths in their respective fields.

Adobe Creative Studio is a suite of powerful tools designed to unleash your creative potential. By learning how to effectively use these applications, you will be well-equipped to bring your ideas to life, refine your skills, and elevate your creative work.

1.2: Exploring the Adobe Creative Studio Suite

Adobe Creative Studio is a collection of industry-leading applications that cater to different aspects of the creative process. These applications are designed to work seamlessly together, enabling you to create stunning visuals, engaging content, and compelling stories. Here's a brief overview of the core applications in the Adobe Creative Studio suite:

Adobe Photoshop: A powerful image editing and manipulation tool that allows you to retouch photos, create composites, and design digital artwork.

Adobe Illustrator: A vector-based illustration program perfect for creating logos, icons, and complex illustrations that can be scaled without losing quality.

Adobe InDesign: A professional layout and publication design tool used to create eye-catching magazines, brochures, eBooks, and more.

Adobe Premiere Pro: A comprehensive video editing and production application for creating captivating films, commercials, and social media content.

Adobe After Effects: A motion graphics and visual effects software used to create animated titles, engaging transitions, and stunning visual effects for video projects.

Additional tools and services in the suite include Adobe Bridge, Creative Cloud Libraries, Adobe Stock, and more, which help streamline your workflow and enhance your creative projects.

1.3: Setting Up Your Workspace

Before diving into the world of Adobe Creative Studio, it's essential to set up your workspace for an efficient and productive creative experience.

System requirements and installation: Ensure your computer meets the minimum system requirements for each application. Visit the Adobe website for detailed information on system requirements and follow the installation process for the Creative Studio suite.

Customizing the interface and workspace: Each Adobe application offers a customizable interface that can be tailored to your preferences. Familiarize yourself with the workspaces, panels, toolbars, and menus in each application, and arrange them according to your workflow. Save your customized workspace layout for future use.

Syncing settings and assets: Adobe Creative Cloud allows you to sync settings, assets, and preferences across devices. This ensures a consistent and seamless experience, whether you're working on a desktop, laptop, or tablet. Sign in to your Adobe Creative Cloud account and enable syncing to take advantage of this feature.

Optimizing your physical workspace: Your physical environment can greatly impact your productivity and creativity. Ensure your workspace is comfortable, well-lit, and free from distractions. Organize your desk, invest in ergonomic furniture, and consider adding inspirational elements like artwork or plants to create a conducive atmosphere for your creative work.

Chapter 2: Adobe Photoshop – Image Editing and Manipulation

2.1: Navigating the Photoshop Interface

Adobe Photoshop is a powerful image editing and manipulation tool used by professionals and hobbyists alike. Before diving into its features, it's crucial to familiarize yourself with the Photoshop interface.

- Workspace: The Photoshop workspace consists of the canvas (where your image is displayed), panels, toolbars, and menus. Panels contain various tools and options, while the toolbar on the left side of the screen contains commonly used tools.
- Menus: The menu bar at the top of the screen provides access to various commands, options, and settings. Menus like File, Edit, Image, Layer, and Filter are essential for managing your work.
- Customization: Photoshop allows you to customize your workspace by dragging, resizing, and rearranging panels. You can also create and save custom workspace layouts to suit your preferences.

2.2: Working with Layers and Selections

Layers and selections are fundamental concepts in Photoshop, as they allow for non-destructive editing and precise control over your work.

- Layers: Layers are like transparent sheets stacked on top of each other, enabling you to work on individual elements without affecting the rest of the image. Layers can be created, deleted, rearranged, and merged to achieve various effects.
- Layer properties: Each layer has properties such as opacity, blending mode, and layer styles that can be adjusted to achieve the desired effect.
- Selections: Selections allow you to isolate specific areas of an image for editing. Photoshop offers several selection tools, such as the Marquee, Lasso, and Magic Wand tools, as well as advanced techniques like Quick Selection and Select and Mask.

2.3: Color Correction and Retouching Techniques

Photoshop offers a wide range of color correction and retouching tools to enhance and perfect your images.

- Adjustments: Use adjustment layers and tools like Levels, Curves, and Hue/Saturation to correct brightness, contrast, and color balance non-destructively.
- Retouching tools: Remove imperfections and unwanted objects with tools like the Spot Healing Brush, Clone Stamp, and Content-Aware Fill.
- Smart Objects: Convert layers into Smart Objects to apply non-destructive transformations and filters, preserving the original image data.

2.4: Creating Composites and Applying Effects

Photoshop allows you to create stunning composites and apply various effects to your images.

- Composites: Combine multiple images using layer masks, blending modes, and adjustment layers to create seamless and realistic composites.
- Layer styles and effects: Add depth and interest to your designs with layer styles such as Drop Shadow, Bevel and Emboss, and Stroke, or apply filters like Blur, Sharpen, and Distort to achieve various effects.
- Smart Filters: Apply filters non-destructively to Smart Objects, allowing for easy adjustments and flexibility.

2.5: Exporting and Optimizing Images

Once your work is complete, it's essential to save and optimize your images for their intended use.

- File formats: Save your images in various formats such as JPEG, PNG, GIF, or TIFF, depending on your needs and the platform where they will be displayed.
- Image resolution and compression: Understand the relationship between image resolution, dimensions, and compression to ensure your images look sharp and load quickly on various devices.
- Exporting: Use the Export As or Save for Web (Legacy) features to save and optimize your images for web, print, or other specific uses.

Chapter 3: Adobe Illustrator – Vector Art and Illustration

Here are some examples of how you might apply the advices from Chapter 3, which focuses on Adobe Illustrator for vector art and illustration, in real-world scenarios:

Example 1: Designing a company logo

Sketch and conceptualize ideas for the logo, considering principles like simplicity, versatility, and memorability.

Use the Pen Tool to create precise and clean vector shapes that form the logo.

Apply appropriate colors, gradients, or patterns to enhance the visual impact of the logo.

If necessary, incorporate typography into the logo using Illustrator's advanced text tools and effects.

Example 2: Creating an infographic for a blog post

Organize the Illustrator workspace to suit the specific needs of the project, such as having panels like Layers, Swatches, and Symbols readily accessible.

Use the Pen and Pencil Tools to draw custom icons, charts, and other graphics that will be part of the infographic.

Apply a cohesive color scheme throughout the infographic using the Swatches panel, and create smooth color transitions with gradients where necessary.

Utilize text effects and OpenType features to create eye-catching headings, subheadings, and data labels.

Example 3: Designing a custom pattern for a product packaging

Begin by sketching a basic pattern concept, considering elements like shape, color, and scale.

Use the Pen, Pencil, or Shape Tools to create the individual vector elements that will make up the pattern.

Experiment with colors, gradients, and patterns to achieve the desired look for each element.

Assemble the pattern in the Pattern Options panel, ensuring that it tiles seamlessly and appears balanced.

Save the pattern as a swatch and apply it to the product packaging design as a fill or stroke.

Example 4: Creating a vector illustration for a children's book

Set up your Illustrator workspace, ensuring that essential panels, like Layers, Brushes, and the Pathfinder panel, are easily accessible.

Use a combination of the Pen Tool and Pencil Tool to draw characters, backgrounds, and other elements in the scene, taking advantage of the unique capabilities of each tool.

Experiment with various colors, gradients, and patterns to bring the illustration to life, ensuring that the color scheme is visually appealing and suitable for the target audience.

If necessary, incorporate text into the illustration using Illustrator's advanced typography tools, such as the Type on a Path Tool and OpenType features.

By applying the advice from Chapter 3 in these examples, you can create visually appealing and professional-quality vector art and illustrations, effectively utilizing the powerful tools and features available in Adobe Illustrator.

3.1: Understanding the Illustrator Workspace

Adobe Illustrator is a powerful vector-based illustration software, perfect for creating scalable graphics such as logos, icons, and complex illustrations. Familiarizing yourself with the Illustrator workspace will help you work more efficiently.

- Workspace: The Illustrator workspace consists of the artboard (where your design is displayed), panels, toolbars, and menus. Panels contain various tools and options, while the toolbar on the left side of the screen houses commonly used tools.
- Menus: The menu bar at the top of the screen provides access to various commands, options, and settings. Essential menus include File, Edit, Object, Type, and Window.
- Customization: Illustrator allows you to customize your workspace by dragging, resizing, and rearranging panels. You can also create and save custom workspace layouts to suit your preferences.

3.2: Drawing with the Pen and Pencil Tools

Illustrator offers various drawing tools for creating and editing paths, which form the basis of vector graphics.

- Pen Tool: The Pen Tool is a versatile and precise drawing tool that allows you to create straight and curved paths by placing anchor points and adjusting direction handles.
- Pencil Tool: The Pencil Tool enables you to draw freeform paths and shapes, giving your illustrations a more organic, hand-drawn feel. The Smooth Tool and Path Eraser Tool can be used to refine your Pencil-drawn paths.

3.3: Working with Colors, Gradients, and Patterns

Colors, gradients, and patterns are essential elements in creating visually appealing vector illustrations.

- Colors: Illustrator offers various ways to apply colors to your artwork, such as the Color Picker, Swatches panel, and Color panel. You can work with different color modes, including RGB, CMYK, and HSB.
- Gradients: Gradients allow you to create smooth transitions between colors. Use the Gradient panel and Gradient Tool to create and edit linear, radial, or freeform gradients.
- Patterns: Patterns can be applied as fills or strokes to create repeating designs. Create your own patterns using the Pattern Options panel, or choose from a library of pre-made patterns.

3.4: Typography and Text Effects

Illustrator provides extensive typography features and text effects to enhance your designs.

- Text tools: Use the Type Tool to create point text, area text, or text on a path. Adjust the font, size, and other type attributes using the Character and Paragraph panels.
- Text effects: Apply various text effects, such as envelope distortions, 3D extrusions, or pattern fills, to create unique and eye-catching typography.

- Converting text to outlines: Convert text to outlines to turn it into editable vector shapes, allowing for more advanced manipulation and customization.

3.5: Designing Logos and Icons

Illustrator is the go-to software for designing scalable logos and icons.

Sketching and conceptualization: Begin by sketching your ideas on paper or using the Pencil Tool in Illustrator. Consider the principles of effective logo design, such as simplicity, versatility, and memorability.

Refining your design: Use the Pen Tool, Shape Tools, and Pathfinder panel to create precise and clean vector shapes. Combine and modify shapes to achieve your desired design.

Final touches: Apply color, gradients, or patterns to your logo or icon, and add any necessary typography. Ensure that your design is visually balanced and effectively communicates the intended message or brand identity.

Chapter 4: Adobe InDesign – Layout and Publication Design

Chapter 4 focuses on Adobe InDesign, which is used for layout and publication design. Here are some examples of how you might apply the advice from this chapter in real-world scenarios:

Example 1: Creating a brochure for a local business

Utilize master pages to set up consistent headers, footers, and background elements throughout the brochure.

Use paragraph and character styles to ensure consistent typography for headings, subheadings, and body text.

Place high-resolution images into frames and apply text wrapping to create a visually appealing layout.

Export the brochure as a print-ready PDF, ensuring that the document has the appropriate bleed and slug settings, as well as using the CMYK color space.

Example 2: Designing a digital magazine

Set up a grid structure using guides to create a consistent and visually appealing layout across multiple pages.

Incorporate interactive elements, such as hyperlinks and buttons, to create a more engaging reading experience for digital audiences.

Ensure the document's accessibility by using clear and legible typography, structuring content with headings and lists, and adding alt text to images.

Export the digital magazine as an interactive PDF or Publish Online document to optimize the reading experience on various devices and platforms.

Example 3: Crafting a professional resume and cover letter

Use the Character and Paragraph Styles to format headings, subheadings, and body text consistently across both the resume and cover letter.

Use columns to create an organized, visually balanced layout for your resume.

Place your personal logo or other branding elements in the header or footer using frames.

Export your resume and cover letter as a print-ready PDF for physical copies or an interactive PDF for digital submission.

In each of these examples, applying the advice from Chapter 4 helps create visually appealing, professional-quality publications while streamlining the design process and ensuring the final product meets the intended purpose.

4.1: An Introduction to InDesign's Interface

Adobe InDesign is a professional layout and publication design software used to create eye-catching print and digital materials. To work efficiently in InDesign, it's essential to familiarize yourself with its interface.

- Workspace: The InDesign workspace consists of the document area (where your layout is displayed), panels, toolbars, and menus. Panels contain various tools and options, while the toolbar on the left side of the screen houses commonly used tools.
- Menus: The menu bar at the top of the screen provides access to various commands, options, and settings. Essential menus include File, Edit, Layout, Type, and Object.
- Customization: InDesign allows you to customize your workspace by dragging, resizing, and rearranging panels. You can also create and save custom workspace layouts to suit your preferences.

4.2: Creating and Managing Pages and Master Pages

Pages and master pages are essential components of any InDesign layout.

- Pages: Use the Pages panel to create, delete, and rearrange pages in your document. InDesign offers various page presets and the ability to customize page size, orientation, and margins.
- Master Pages: Master pages serve as templates for the layout and design elements that appear consistently throughout your document. Apply master pages to multiple document pages to ensure consistent formatting and easily make global changes.

4.3: Working with Text, Frames, and Graphics

InDesign offers various tools and features for working with text, frames, and graphics.

- Frames: Frames are containers for text or graphics and can be created using the Text Tool or Rectangle Frame Tool. Use the Selection Tool to resize, move, and rotate frames, or use the Direct Selection Tool to adjust frame paths.
- Placing content: Place text or graphics into frames by choosing File > Place or using the keyboard shortcut Ctrl+D (Cmd+D on Mac). InDesign supports a wide range of file formats, including PSD, AI, JPEG, and PDF.
- Wrapping text: Use the Text Wrap panel to control how text flows around graphics or other objects in your layout.

4.4: Typography and Styling in InDesign

InDesign provides advanced typography and styling features to enhance your layouts.

- Character and Paragraph Styles: Create and apply character and paragraph styles to ensure consistent formatting throughout your document. Styles allow you to easily update text formatting across your entire document with just a few clicks.
- OpenType features: InDesign supports advanced OpenType features, such as ligatures, swashes, and stylistic sets, which can be accessed through the Character panel or the OpenType panel.
- Columns and grids: Use columns and grids to create organized, visually appealing layouts. InDesign offers various tools for creating and managing column and grid structures, including the Layout > Margins and Columns command and the Create Guides feature.

4.5: Preparing Files for Print and Digital Publishing

Once your layout is complete, it's essential to prepare your files for print or digital publishing.

- Preflight: Use the Preflight panel to check your document for potential issues, such as missing fonts or overset text. InDesign's preflight feature helps you identify and resolve problems before exporting your final file.
- Packaging: Choose File > Package to gather all necessary files, such as linked graphics and fonts, into a single folder. This ensures that your document will display and print correctly on other computers or when sent to a print service provider.
- Exporting: Export your document in the appropriate format for its intended use. For print projects, choose File > Export and select Adobe PDF (Print) as the file format. For digital publishing, choose File > Export and select Adobe PDF (Interactive) or another suitable format, such as EPUB or Publish Online. Each format offers various options and settings to ensure optimal display and performance on different devices and platforms.
- Print settings: When exporting for print, pay close attention to settings like color space (CMYK for print, RGB for digital), resolution, and bleed and slug areas. It's crucial to

consult with your print service provider to ensure your document meets their specific requirements.

- Accessibility: When preparing your document for digital publishing, consider accessibility features, such as adding alt text for images, using clear and legible typography, and structuring your content with headings and lists. This ensures that your document can be easily navigated and understood by all readers, including those using assistive technologies.

By understanding and utilizing InDesign's powerful layout and design capabilities, you can create professional, visually engaging publications that effectively communicate your message and leave a lasting impression on your audience.

Chapter 5: Adobe Premiere Pro – Video Editing and Production

Here are some examples of how you might apply the advice from Chapter 5, which focuses on Adobe Premiere Pro for video editing and production, in real-world scenarios:

Example 1: Creating a promotional video for a product

Import footage of the product, interviews, testimonials, and relevant images or graphics into Premiere Pro.

Organize your media assets into bins by type or scene, such as "Product Shots," "Interviews," or "B-roll."

Assemble your video in the Timeline panel, layering and synchronizing clips to create a cohesive narrative.

Apply transitions between clips for smooth scene changes and use video effects to enhance the visual appeal of your footage.

Add text titles and lower-thirds to emphasize key messages and introduce speakers.

Export the video using a preset optimized for your target platform, such as YouTube or Vimeo.

Example 2: Editing a short film

Import all the raw footage, audio files, and any additional media assets, such as music or sound effects.

Organize the assets in the Project panel, creating bins for each scene or location.

Assemble the film in the Timeline panel, using multiple tracks to layer video and audio elements, and fine-tune the timing and pacing of each scene.

Apply color correction using the Lumetri Color panel to achieve a consistent look and feel across the entire film.

Add titles or credits using the Essential Graphics panel.

Export the film in the desired format, considering the intended distribution channels and audience.

Example 3: Producing a tutorial or educational video

Import screen recordings, voiceover audio, and any additional media assets, such as images or graphics.

Organize your assets into bins, separating them by topic or section of the tutorial.

Assemble the video in the Timeline panel, synchronizing the voiceover audio with the screen recordings and any additional visuals.

Apply audio effects, such as equalization or noise reduction, to improve the quality of the voiceover

Use text titles or annotations to emphasize key points or instructions.

Export the video using a preset tailored for online platforms or e-learning environments.

By applying the advice from Chapter 5 in these examples, you can create visually appealing and professional-quality videos, effectively utilizing the powerful tools and features available in Adobe Premiere Pro.

5.1: Exploring the Premiere Pro Workspace

Adobe Premiere Pro is a powerful and versatile video editing software used by professionals and amateurs alike. To work efficiently in Premiere Pro, it's essential to familiarize yourself with its interface.

- Workspace: The Premiere Pro workspace consists of panels, such as the Project, Source, Program, Timeline, and Tools panels. These panels provide you with various tools, options, and controls for editing your video.
- Customization: Premiere Pro allows you to customize your workspace by rearranging, resizing, and docking panels. You can also save custom workspace layouts to suit your preferences and switch between them as needed.

5.2: Importing and Organizing Media

Before you start editing, you'll need to import your media files into Premiere Pro and organize them effectively.

- Importing: Use the File > Import command, the Media Browser panel, or simply drag and drop files into the Project panel to import media.
- Organizing: Create bins in the Project panel to organize your media assets, such as video clips, audio files, and images. Use descriptive names and labels to help you easily locate assets during the editing process.

5.3: Basic Editing Techniques and Transitions

Once your media is imported and organized, you can begin editing your video in the Timeline pane

- Timeline: The Timeline panel is where you arrange, edit, and trim your video clips. You can create multiple tracks for video and audio, allowing you to layer and synchronize your media.
- Cutting and trimming: Use the Razor Tool to cut clips, and the Selection Tool to trim and extend clips by dragging their edges.
- Transitions: Add transitions, such as cross-dissolve or wipe, between clips to create smooth, seamless scene changes. Use the Effects panel to access a variety of pre-built transitions.

5.4: Adding Titles, Effects, and Color Correction

Enhance your video with titles, effects, and color correction to create a polished, professional look.

- Titles: Use the Essential Graphics panel to create and customize text titles, lower-thirds, and other graphics. You can also import graphics from Adobe Illustrator or Adobe Photoshop.
- Effects: Apply video and audio effects, such as stabilization, blur, or equalization, from the Effects panel to enhance your footage and audio.
- Color correction: Use the Lumetri Color panel to adjust the color balance, exposure, and saturation of your video clips, achieving a consistent and cinematic look across your entire project.

5.5: Exporting and Sharing Your Videos

Once your video is edited and polished, export it in the appropriate format for sharing or distribution.

- Export Settings: Choose File > Export > Media to open the Export Settings dialog. Select the desired format and codec, adjust the resolution, frame rate, and bitrate, and choose the output location for your video file.
- Presets: Premiere Pro provides numerous export presets for popular platforms like YouTube, Vimeo, and Facebook, ensuring optimal quality and compatibility.
- Review and Export: Use the Source and Output previews in the Export Settings dialog to review your video and ensure everything is correct before exporting.

By understanding and utilizing Premiere Pro's powerful video editing and production capabilities, you can create professional-quality videos that effectively convey your message and engage your audience.

Chapter 6: Adobe After Effects – Motion Graphics and Visual Effects

Here are some examples of how you might apply the advice from Chapter 6, which focuses on Adobe After Effects for motion graphics and visual effects, in real-world scenarios:

Example 1: Creating an animated explainer video

Import assets, such as vector illustrations, background images, and voiceover audio into After Effects.

Organize your assets into folders in the Project panel for easy access.

Create animations using keyframes to move, scale, rotate, and change the opacity of the elements in your scene.

Apply effects like drop shadows or glows to enhance the visuals and make the elements stand out.

Use 3D layers and cameras to create depth and perspective, making your animations more engaging and immersive.

Render and export your explainer video in the appropriate format for your target platform, such as YouTube or a presentation.

Example 2: Designing a title sequence for a film or series

Import any necessary assets, such as video clips, images, or logos.

Create text layers for the film or series title, as well as any additional credits or information.

Animate the text layers using keyframes, experimenting with position, scale, rotation, and opacity to create dynamic and engaging animations.

Apply visual effects, such as glows, particle systems, or distortion effects, to enhance the title sequence's impact.

If appropriate, use 3D layers and cameras to add depth and create more complex animations.

Render and export your title sequence to be integrated into the final video project.

Example 3: Compositing visual effects for a video project

Import the original video footage and any additional elements, such as 3D renders, images, or stock footage, into After Effects.

Use layers and masks to blend the elements seamlessly, adjusting opacity, feathering, or using blending modes.

Apply visual effects, such as color correction, lens flares, or particle systems, to enhance the scene and create a cohesive look.

Track and match any camera movements in the original footage using 3D layers and cameras.

Render and export the composited video to be integrated back into the main video project.

By applying the advices from Chapter 6 in these examples, you can create visually engaging and professional-quality motion graphics and visual effects, effectively utilizing the powerful tools and features available in Adobe After Effects.

6.1: Navigating the After Effects Interface

Adobe After Effects is a powerful tool for creating motion graphics, visual effects, and compositing. To work effectively in After Effects, it's essential to familiarize yourself with its interface.

- Workspace: The After Effects workspace consists of panels, such as the Project, Composition, Timeline, and Effects & Presets panels. These panels provide you with various tools, options, and controls for creating and editing your projects.
- Customization: After Effects allows you to customize your workspace by rearranging, resizing, and docking panels. You can also save custom workspace layouts to suit your preferences and switch between them as needed.

6.2: Working with Layers and Keyframes

After Effects uses layers and keyframes to create animations and apply effects.

- Layers: Similar to Photoshop and Illustrator, After Effects uses layers to organize and combine different elements in your project. Layers can be various media types, such as video, images, text, or even audio.
- Keyframes: Keyframes are used to define the starting and ending points of an animation or effect. You can set keyframes for any property, such as position, scale, or opacity, to create smooth transitions between values over time.

6.3: Creating Basic Animations and Effects

Create visually engaging animations and apply a wide range of effects using After Effects.

- Animation: Use keyframes to animate layer properties, such as position, scale, rotation, and opacity. Experiment with the Graph Editor to fine-tune your animations and achieve the desired motion and timing.
- Effects: The Effects & Presets panel offers a vast library of built-in effects that you can apply to your layers, such as blurs, glows, and distortion effects. Combine multiple effects to create unique and interesting visuals.

6.4: Using 3D Layers and Cameras

Enhance your projects with 3D layers and camera movements for a more dynamic and immersive experience.

- 3D Layers: Convert 2D layers into 3D layers to enable additional properties, such as Z-axis position and rotation. Arrange 3D layers in 3D space to create depth and perspective.
- Cameras: Create virtual cameras to navigate the 3D space and control the viewer's perspective. Animate camera properties, such as position, rotation, and zoom, to create dynamic camera movements and transitions.

6.5: Rendering and Exporting Your Projects

Once your project is complete, render and export it in the appropriate format for sharing or distribution.

- Render Queue: Use the Render Queue panel to set up and manage the rendering of your compositions. Choose the desired output module settings, such as format, codec, and resolution, and specify the output location for your rendered files.
- Export Settings: You can also export your projects directly from After Effects using Adobe Media Encoder, which offers additional presets and options for various platforms and devices.
- Preview and Render: Use the Preview panel to review your project and ensure everything is correct before rendering and exporting.

By understanding and utilizing After Effects' powerful motion graphics and visual effects capabilities, you can create engaging and professional-quality projects that captivate your audience.

Chapter 7: Integrating Adobe Creative Studio Applications

Here are some examples of how you might apply the advice from Chapter 7, which focuses on integrating Adobe Creative Studio applications, in real-world scenarios:

Example 1: Designing a marketing campaign

Create a Creative Cloud Library for your marketing campaign, adding assets such as brand colors, logos, fonts, and images.

Access the library from different Adobe applications, such as Photoshop, Illustrator, or InDesign, to maintain consistency across your campaign materials.

Use Adobe Bridge to browse, preview, and organize your campaign assets, applying metadata and keywords for easy access and searchability.

Collaborate with your team members using Adobe Team Projects to create a cohesive and consistent marketing campaign, sharing progress and updates in real-time.

Example 2: Producing a video series with motion graphics

Store and sync assets such as video clips, audio files, images, and graphics using Creative Cloud Libraries, ensuring all team members have access to the latest versions.

Collaborate with your team members on editing the video series using Adobe Team Projects in Premiere Pro, allowing for real-time updates and version control.

Integrate motion graphics created in After Effects by accessing the shared Creative Cloud Library, ensuring consistent visuals and branding across the video series.

Use Adobe Bridge to manage and organize your assets, streamlining your workflow and making it easier to locate the files you need throughout the production process.

Example 3: Creating a multimedia presentation

Build a Creative Cloud Library for your presentation, including elements such as company logos, branded colors, and fonts.

Access your library from various Adobe applications like Photoshop, Illustrator, and InDesign, ensuring a cohesive design across all presentation materials.

Collaborate with team members on the presentation using Adobe Team Projects, allowing multiple users to work simultaneously on the same project file.

Employ Adobe Bridge to preview, organize, and manage your presentation assets, including images, graphics, and PDF documents.

By applying the advice from Chapter 7 in these examples, you can create a seamless and efficient workflow, leveraging the powerful integration features of Adobe Creative Studio applications to work effectively across multiple projects and with your team members.

7.1: Syncing Assets with Creative Cloud Libraries

Adobe Creative Cloud Libraries allow you to store, manage, and sync assets across multiple applications within the Adobe Creative Studio suite.

- Creating Libraries: Create a new Creative Cloud Library in any compatible Adobe application, such as Photoshop, Illustrator, or After Effects. You can create libraries for specific projects, clients, or themes.
- Adding Assets: Add assets to your libraries, including colors, text styles, images, graphics, or even videos. You can access and use these assets in any Adobe application that supports Creative Cloud Libraries.
- Syncing and Sharing: Creative Cloud Libraries automatically sync across your devices and Adobe applications, ensuring you have access to the latest versions of your assets. You can also share libraries with team members, allowing for easy collaboration.

7.2: Collaborating with Adobe Team Projects

Adobe Team Projects is a powerful collaboration tool that enables multiple users to work simultaneously on a project within Premiere Pro, After Effects, or other Adobe applications.

- Creating a Team Project: Start a new Team Project or convert an existing project to a Team Project in the File menu of your Adobe application. Invite your team members to join the project using their Adobe IDs.
- Collaborative Editing: Work simultaneously on the same project with your team members. Team Projects uses version control and conflict resolution to manage changes and prevent overwriting of work.
- Sharing Changes: Use the Share Changes button to sync your work with the team project, allowing others to access your latest edits and updates.

7.3: Streamlining Your Workflow with Adobe Bridge

Adobe Bridge is a versatile asset management application that helps you stay organized and streamline your workflow across Adobe Creative Studio applications.

- Browsing and Previewing: Browse and preview your assets, such as images, videos, audio files, and Adobe project files, within Adobe Bridge. You can also access metadata, keywords, and other information related to your assets.
- Organizing: Use Adobe Bridge to create folders, add keywords, and apply labels or ratings t your assets, making it easier to locate and access them when needed.
- Batch Processing: Utilize Adobe Bridge's batch processing features, such as batch renaming resizing, or applying metadata, to streamline your workflow and save time.

By integrating Adobe Creative Studio applications using Creative Cloud Libraries, Adobe Team Projects, and Adobe Bridge, you can create a seamless and efficient workflow that allows you to work more effectively across multiple projects and with your team members.

Chapter 8: Essential Tips and Tricks for Creative Success

Here are some examples of how you might apply the advice from Chapter 8, which focuses on essential tips and tricks for creative success, in real-world scenarios:

Example 1: Working on a graphic design project

Learn and use keyboard shortcuts for frequently used tools in Adobe Photoshop, Illustrator, or InDesign, such as selection tools, layers, and color adjustments.

Organize your design files using a consistent naming convention, like "ProjectName_DesignElement_Version," and create a clear folder structure for storing assets, working files, and final exports.

Participate in online forums and Adobe community platforms to seek feedback on your work, ask questions, and share knowledge with other designers.

Example 2: Creating an animated explainer video

Customize keyboard shortcuts in Adobe After Effects or Premiere Pro to better suit your personal workflow and preferences, speeding up your editing and animation process.

Develop a systematic organization method for your video project files, separating source assets, project files, and final exports in distinct folders.

Watch online tutorials and attend webinars on topics such as motion graphics, animation technique or video editing to expand your skillset and stay up to date with industry trends.

Example 3: Designing a website or mobile app

Utilize keyboard shortcuts in Adobe XD or other Adobe applications to quickly access tools, functions, and commands, streamlining your design workflow.

Create an organized file management system for your web or app design project, using a consistent naming convention and folder structure for your design files, assets, and exported prototypes.

Engage with the Adobe community on social media and forums to ask questions, seek inspiration, and share your work, helping you learn from others and stay motivated in your design process.

By applying the advice from Chapter 8 in these examples, you can improve your workflow, stay organized, and continue to learn and grow as a creative professional. Embrace the essential tips and tricks to make the most out of Adobe Creative Studio applications and achieve creative success in your projects.

8.1: Keyboard Shortcuts and Customization

Keyboard shortcuts and customization can greatly improve your efficiency and workflow in Adobe Creative Studio applications.

- Learn Default Shortcuts: Familiarize yourself with the default keyboard shortcuts for frequently used tools, functions, and commands in each application.
- Customize Shortcuts: Customize your keyboard shortcuts to match your preferences or to better align with your workflow. You can find the keyboard shortcut settings in the preferences of each Adobe application.
- Save Time: Utilize keyboard shortcuts to perform tasks more quickly, freeing up more time for creative work and experimentation.

8.2: Staying Organized and Managing Files

Effectively organizing and managing your files is crucial for maintaining an efficient workflow and preventing issues down the road.

- Naming Conventions: Develop a consistent naming convention for your files, including versions and iterations, to make it easy to locate specific files and understand their contents.
- Folder Structure: Create a logical folder structure for your projects, organizing assets, working files, and final exports in a clear and consistent manner.
- File Formats: Save your files in appropriate formats, ensuring compatibility and quality for their intended use. Keep editable source files separate from final exported files to avoid accidental overwriting or loss of work.

8.3: Learning from the Adobe Community

The Adobe community is a valuable resource for learning, inspiration, and problem-solving.

- Tutorials and Guides: Take advantage of the vast library of tutorials and guides available online, including those on the official Adobe website and on platforms such as YouTube. These resources can help you learn new techniques, troubleshoot issues, or expand your creative skillset.

- Forums and Social Media: Engage with other Adobe users on forums, social media, or dedicated community platforms. Share your work, ask questions, and learn from the experiences and knowledge of others.
- Creative Inspiration: Stay inspired by browsing the work of other creatives, attending webinars or conferences, and participating in design challenges or contests. This can help you stay motivated, learn new techniques, and discover trends within the industry.

By incorporating these essential tips and tricks into your daily workflow, you can improve your efficiency, stay organized, and continue to learn and grow as a creative professional. Embrace the power of Adobe Creative Studio applications and the broader Adobe community to achieve creative success.

Chapter 9: Building Your Creative Portfolio

Here are some examples of how you might apply the advice from Chapter 9, which focuses on building your creative portfolio, in real-world scenarios:

Example 1: Graphic Designer

Curate a selection of your best graphic design projects, such as branding, packaging, print, and digital design work, showcasing your range of skills and versatility.

Develop a consistent visual identity for your portfolio, including colors, typography, and layout that reflect your personal style and creative approach.

Create a professional website using Adobe Portfolio and showcase your projects on Behance, engaging with other designers and participating in curated galleries to increase your visibility.

Example 2: Photographer

Choose your strongest photographs that demonstrate your technical skills, artistic eye, and unique style, focusing on a diverse range of subjects and styles.

Tailor your portfolio to suit the needs and expectations of your target audience, such as potential clients, galleries, or publishers, by including relevant work and a clear description of your photography services.

Share your work on both Adobe Portfolio and Behance, networking with other photographers, participating in industry events, and seeking feedback to refine your photography skills.

Example 3: Motion Graphics Artist

Include a variety of motion graphics projects in your portfolio, such as animated explainer videos, title sequences, and commercial spots, demonstrating your ability to create compelling visuals for different purposes and audiences.

Arrange your projects in a meaningful order, telling a story of your growth and development as a motion graphics artist.

Leverage Adobe Portfolio to build a responsive website showcasing your work, and share your projects on Behance to connect with other motion graphics professionals, gain feedback, and discover job opportunities.

By applying the advices from Chapter 9 in these examples, you can create a compelling and effective creative portfolio that showcases your skills, personal style, and experience. Embrace the power of Adobe Portfolio and Behance to reach a wider audience, network with other creatives, and achieve your professional goals.

9.1: Curating Your Best Work

A well-curated creative portfolio is essential for showcasing your skills, experience, and personal style to potential clients or employers.

- Quality Over Quantity: Select only your strongest work for your portfolio, focusing on projects that demonstrate your technical skills, creative problem-solving abilities, and unique style.
- Variety: Include a diverse range of projects in your portfolio to showcase your versatility and adaptability. However, ensure that the work you include is still relevant to the type of work you want to be hired for.
- Context and Process: Provide context for each project by including a brief description of the project's goals, challenges, and outcomes. Additionally, consider sharing your creative process, sketches, or iterations to give insight into your working methods.

9.2: Showcasing Your Skills and Style

Your portfolio should effectively communicate your skills and personal style as a creative professional.

- Consistent Branding: Develop a consistent visual identity for your portfolio, incorporating elements such as color schemes, typography, and layout to create a cohesive and professional appearance.
- Tailored Presentations: Tailor your portfolio to suit the specific needs and expectations of your target audience, whether it's a potential client or employer. This may involve customizing your portfolio for different industries or job roles.
- Storytelling: Tell a story with your portfolio by arranging your projects in a meaningful order, such as chronologically, by theme, or by the complexity of the work. This can help guide viewers through your creative journey and demonstrate your growth over time.

9.3: Leveraging Adobe Portfolio and Behance

Adobe offers powerful tools for building and showcasing your creative portfolio, such as Adobe Portfolio and Behance.

- Adobe Portfolio: Use Adobe Portfolio to create a professional, customizable, and responsive website to showcase your work. Choose from a variety of templates and easily integrate your projects from other Adobe applications and services.
- Behance: Join the Behance community to share your work, network with other creatives, and discover job opportunities. Upload projects to your Behance profile and participate in curated galleries, challenges, and industry events to gain exposure and feedback.
- Cross-Promotion: Leverage both Adobe Portfolio and Behance to reach a wider audience and maximize your exposure. Promote your work on social media and other online platforms to increase your visibility and attract potential clients or employers.

By carefully curating your best work, showcasing your skills and personal style, and leveraging Adobe Portfolio and Behance, you can build a compelling creative portfolio that stands out from the competition and helps you achieve your professional goals.

Chapter 10: Taking Your Creative Skills to the Next Level

Here are some examples of how you might apply the advice from Chapter 10, which focuses on taking your creative skills to the next level, in real-world scenarios:

Example 1: Web Designer

Experiment with new web design trends and techniques, such as responsive design, interactive elements, or accessibility features, to create innovative and user-friendly websites.

Take online courses or attend workshops on advanced web design tools, such as Adobe XD, to stay up to date with the latest features and functionalities.

Attend industry events or join professional organizations, such as AIGA or Webflow Community, to network with other web designers and gain insights into the latest trends and best practices in the field.

Example 2: Digital Illustrator

Push yourself to try new styles, techniques, and mediums to expand your creative range and develop a unique voice as an artist.

Take advanced training sessions or online courses on digital illustration tools and techniques, such as Adobe Illustrator or Procreate, to refine your skills and create more complex and sophisticated illustrations.

Seek mentorship from experienced illustrators or participate in online critique groups to gain feedback and insights on your work, and refine your creative process.

Example 3: Video Editor

Stay up to date with the latest video editing trends and techniques, such as color grading, motion graphics, or VR editing, to create compelling and impactful videos.

Attend workshops or online courses on advanced video editing tools, such as Adobe Premiere Pro or DaVinci Resolve, to deepen your technical skills and improve your workflow.

Join professional organizations, such as the National Association of Broadcasters or the Motion Graphics Association, to network with other video editors and learn from industry experts.

By applying the advice from Chapter 10 in these examples, you can develop your creative skills, stay up to date with industry trends, and advance your career as a creative professional. Embrace the power of experimentation, education, and networking to take your skills to the next level and achieve your professional goals.

10.1: Exploring Advanced Techniques and Tools

As a creative professional, it's important to continually push yourself to learn new techniques and master advanced tools to stay ahead of the competition.

- Experimentation: Take risks and experiment with new techniques, tools, and approaches to your work. This can help you expand your skillset, discover new creative possibilities, and differentiate your work from others.
- Advanced Training: Attend workshops, online courses, or advanced training sessions to learn more about advanced techniques and tools in Adobe Creative Studio applications. This can help you stay up to date with the latest industry standards and improve your workflow.
- Mentorship: Seek mentorship from experienced professionals in your field, who can provide guidance, feedback, and support in your creative journey.

10.2: Keeping Up with Industry Trends

The creative industry is constantly evolving, and it's important to stay up to date with the latest trends and best practices.

- Research: Stay informed about the latest trends in your industry by reading blogs, magazines, attending conferences or webinars, and following thought leaders and influencers on social media.
- Adaptability: Be adaptable and flexible in your work, being able to pivot to new trends or emerging technologies. This can help you stay relevant and desirable to clients or employers.
- Innovation: Use industry trends and emerging technologies as inspiration for your work, experimenting with new techniques and tools to create innovative and impactful projects.

10.3: Continuing Your Education and Professional Development

Continuing your education and professional development is essential for staying ahead of the curve in your career.

- Formal Education: Pursue formal education opportunities, such as degree programs, online courses, or certifications, to deepen your knowledge and skills in your field.

- Skill Development: Take advantage of training opportunities in Adobe Creative Studio applications, such as online tutorials or live workshops, to refine your skills and stay up to date with the latest features and tools.
- Networking: Build a network of like-minded professionals and attend industry events, conferences, or meetups to learn from others, make connections, and seek out job opportunities.

By exploring advanced techniques and tools, keeping up with industry trends, and continuing your education and professional development, you can take your creative skills to the next level and achieve greater success in your career. Embrace a growth mindset and be open to learning new skill and approaches to your work.

Glossary

Adobe Creative Studio: A collection of industry-standard creative applications developed by Adobe Systems, including Photoshop, Illustrator, InDesign, Premiere Pro, After Effects, and more.

Asset: Any digital file, such as images, videos, or audio files, used in a creative project.

Behance: An online platform developed by Adobe Systems for showcasing and discovering creativ work, connecting with other creatives, and seeking out job opportunities.

Bridge: A digital asset management application developed by Adobe Systems for organizing and browsing files across multiple Creative Studio applications.

Creative Cloud Libraries: A cloud-based feature of Adobe Creative Studio that allows users to save and share assets and design elements across multiple projects and applications.

Keyframe: In animation, a keyframe is a frame in which a specific element or property of an animation is set. These keyframes are then used to create a smooth animation between frames.

Layer: A separate level in an image or design file that allows for individual editing and manipulation.

Master Page: In Adobe InDesign, a master page is a template that can be used to apply consistent formatting and design elements across multiple pages.

Pen Tool: A tool in Adobe Illustrator used to create precise vector paths and shapes.

RGB: A color model used in digital design that stands for red, green, and blue. RGB colors are created by combining varying levels of these three primary colors.

Typography: The art and technique of arranging type, including selecting typefaces, point sizes, lin lengths, line-spacing, and letter-spacing.

Vector: A graphic file format that uses mathematical formulas to create smooth, scalable images without pixelation or loss of quality.

Workflow: The process of completing a task or project, including the steps and tools used to accomplish it. A good workflow maximizes efficiency and productivity.

www.ingramcontent.com/pod-product-compliance
Lightning Source LLC
LaVergne TN
LVHW051651050326
832903LV00034B/4812